ENDORSEMENTS

"Sharing knowledge and learning are social activities. Dr. Patricia Pedraza-Nafziger shows how the combination of sound KM fundamentals and social media will improve the exchange of knowledge to accelerate learning. Leaders are provided with practical examples of what is needed to drive engagement across generations. The 7 Fundamentals to Create and Sustain a Successful Knowledge Sharing Organization provides a wake-up call for smart leaders to leverage and grow their experts while retaining young talent."

— **Cindy Hubert**, Executive Director of Client Solutions, **American Productivity and Quality Center (APQC)**, and Author of **The New Edge in Knowledge: How KM is Changing the Way We Do Business**

"Patricia leads the reader into a forest of issues associated with workforce social networking, and out the other side, to knowledge sharing benefits that can shine on a corporation if these seven fundamentals are addressed; she accomplishes this using candid inputs from actual practitioners."

— **Tim Bridges**, former Knowledge Management Executive, and Contributing Author to **Project Management Institute (PMI)** and **Harvard Business Review (HBR).**

The 7 Fundamentals to Create and Sustain a Successful Knowledge Sharing Organization

by

Patricia Pedraza-Nafziger, Ph.D.

For more information contact
www.PatriciaPedrazaNafziger.com

Cover design by Patricia Pedraza-Nafziger.

The 7 Fundamentals to Create and Sustain a Successful Knowledge Sharing Organization: A collection of valuable findings from an aerospace industry case study

Paperback ISBN: 9780989904223
eBook ISBN-13: 978-0-98990

CONTENTS

"Millennials expect to create a better future, using the collaborative power of digital technology."

Mal Fletcher, Media Commentator,
Author, Business Leadership Consultant

INTRODUCTION

Corporate executives must anticipate how trends in business, society, technology, and information converge to change where, when, why, and with whom we work[1]. Within their organizations, corporate leaders have begun to implement media-enabled knowledge sharing strategies[2] to encourage workplace learning and knowledge sharing[3]. As such digital business strategies continue to evolve, corporate leaders and information technology professionals need to understand how knowledge sharing/management affects innovation, productivity, and collaboration in today's multigenerational workforce. Leaders need to be aware that promoting employee collaboration through social networking[4] brings with it potential challenges such as knowledge hoarding and the effects of globalization, i.e., geographic dispersal resulting in borders between departments and locations. Such barriers can impede employee communication and information sharing.

Social media platforms and tools allow individuals, groups, or organizations the ability to engage in social networking, defined as interacting or networking with others online exclusive to a selected community or network. Existing literature primarily focuses on social networking strategies for business-to-business (B2B) or business-to-customer (B2C) marketing[5]. Yet, little literature surrounds how the workforce uses social media within a global company to enhance knowledge sharing, retention, and retrieval; thus the necessity for this case study.

Researchers are beginning to explore social media systems, whether developed internally or off-the-shelf, that are designed to help workers share and retain information. As a result of this study, seven key components necessary to create and sustain a successful knowledge sharing organization were identified:

1. Social "Collaborative" Networking. Today, corporations are challenged to develop creative strategies to make the knowledge of more experienced, often older, employees more accessible to newer, less experienced employees. Corporate executives are showing increased interest in using social networking as a new model of communication for workforce collaboration and knowledge sharing. This interest is motivated by shifts in the workforce due to such events as resignations, retirements, restructuring, outsourcing, and layoffs[6]. These same factors also contribute to employee resistance and job security anxiety[7], which must be dealt with proactively in order to promote the desired knowledge sharing.

2. Virtual Communities of Practice (VCoP). A group of people working together online regarding similar interests or purposes, constitutes a VCoP. Participation in said group tends to promote shared learning and increased understanding among members[8]. For example, the development of a standard practice template among similar, but physically or organizationally separated groups, could be a valuable task for a VCoP.

3. Organizational Learning. Scholars have been studying the link between organizational learning and improvements in corporate functions and activities. Organizational learning depends on both individual and team learning[9.] It can happen both in person and online.

According to Kroon et al., the participation of workforce dialogue and inquiry directly relates to learning on the job; engagement in social media could stimulate work-related learning[10]. Crowdsourcing, for example, is a technique for involving a wide group of individuals in a task by announcing the task online in an open call to participate; this type of internal corporate social networking is slowly increasing[11]. Rapid development of crowdsourcing as a strategy for information retrieval continues to offer new ideas as well as challenges to traditional methods of designing, training, and evaluating information retrieval systems[12].

4. Leadership Priorities. Many corporations have either failed to anticipate the current generational shift or were unable to establish a plan that works. They now struggle to find strategic methodologies to improve knowledge sharing communications and collaboration technology. Although conventional communication tools and approaches are still part of the strategic arsenal, newer and evolving possibilities such as social networking offer progressively more insightful communication methods.

5. Data Security is a principle corporate concern. Mandatory information security training must be required for all employees. Corporate data security policies and procedures must be unambiguous from the employee's viewpoint with regard to establishing the security needed for specific types of employee information sharing. Relevant security options should not be open to interpretation, but rather clearly defined for users. While participating in social networking groups default security selections may relieve user anxiety and promote the deployment and acceptance of information sharing.

6. Training the Workforce. Contemporary research has shown that employee values and preferences differ among the generational cohorts in today's workforce[13]. The new hires, most likely the youngest, are already adapting to communication through social media. More experienced, probably older employees tend to favor more conventional means of communication such as e-mail, cell phones, and instant messaging. The transition from conventional, one-to-one communication to less familiar forums such as social networking groups is not a simple undertaking[14]. The types of communication and collaboration tools used in the workplace are thus being re-evaluated to accommodate the needs of a changing workforce.

7. Knowledge Sharing. Knowledge development, capture, and sharing are requirements for enhancing the innovation and performance of organizations today[15]. Developing an efficient knowledge sharing process requires time, patience, and a willingness among workforce members to share knowledge. To encourage employees to share the knowledge gained through experience requires building trust and an understanding of how their knowledge will be used. Developing an open culture of communication and encouraging confidence through mentorship may help eliminate workforce knowledge hoarding[16]; collaborative online social networking can help achieve this goal.

The theoretical lens of this case study focused on social network theory, process virtualization theory, and organizational learning theory, all of which have contributed significantly to the literature of corporate knowledge sharing and social networking, as identified in Figure 1.

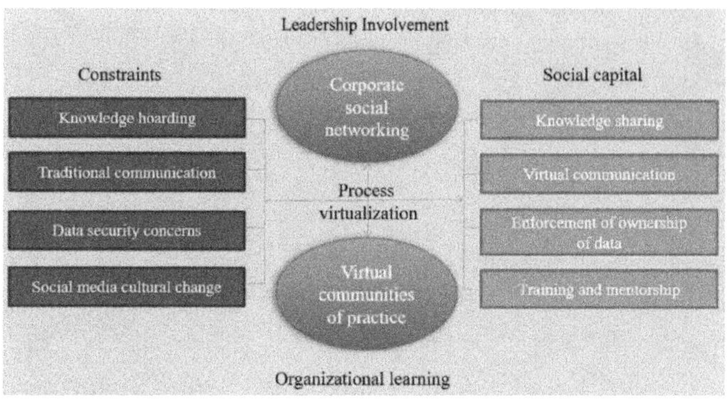

Figure 1. Theoretical framework for the study.

The 7 Fundamentals to Create and Sustain a Successful Knowledge Sharing Organization reports findings discovered through a multinational corporation, referred to for purposes of this study as "Aerospace Inc.," specializing in the design, manufacture, and delivery of aerospace products. This study explores an internally developed social networking tool, referred to as "Enterprise SocNet," used by Aerospace Inc., to deliver online collaboration capabilities to U.S. employees, International employees, contractors, and partners. This research used a qualitative intrinsic case study design that collected data from in-depth semi-structured interviews from group leaders of the most interactive VCoPs using Enterprise SocNet, and artifacts and reports surrounding the purpose and capabilities of Enterprise SocNet. This case study substantiates several vital areas that reflect on how the use of corporate social networking as a centralized source of communication among various VCoPs can help build a more efficient and competitive company.

DEFINITION OF TERMS

Baby Boomers are the population, born between 1946 and 1964, in the years following World War II.

Case Study is an in-depth investigation of a 'single case,' using multiple methods and multiple sources of data[66].

Crowdsourcing. A strategy used to increase education and innovation within and between organizations. Schlagwein and Bjørn-Andersen defined *crowdsourcing* as "online activity in which an individual, an institution, or a company proposes to a group of individuals of varying knowledge, heterogeneity, and number, via a flexible open call, the voluntary undertaking of a task[65]."

Generation X is the population following Baby Boomers, born between 1965 and 1980.

Globalization. The geographic dispersion of organizations, national or international, to promote the ability to conduct business globally.

Enterprise SocNet is the proprietary workforce social networking tool developed by a systems development group at Aerospace Inc., and dedicated to improving workforce collaboration and knowledge sharing.

Internet. Open public space allowing anyone connected to share and access all the information that they choose to via the web.

Intranet. Private space allowing people who are directly wired to the intranet to access the information stored on its servers such as within a corporate environment.

Knowledge hoarding. An activity in which employees who acquire knowledge choose not to share it with coworkers, with the goal of enhancing personal benefit or preserving the knowledge for future use[7].

Knowledge sharing is an activity in which communities, organizations, and coworkers exchange knowledge.

Millennial. Also known as Generation Y, is a person reaching adulthood in the early 21st century, born between 1981 and 2000.

Organization is a group of people supporting a particular business purpose, society, or association.

Process Virtualization. Processes once conducted in a brick-and-mortar environment are now undertaken virtually.

Social Capital is networks of relationships among people who work in a particular group enable them to function more effectively.

Social media is a website or application platform that enables members of a group or forum to create and share or participate in social networking.

Social networking. The use of interactive online applications (often social media platforms) to find, connect and interact with others who share similar interests. Social networking has permeated people's day-to-day lives, becoming an important avenue of computer-mediated communication[18].

Traditional Generation is also referred to as the Silent Generation, born before 1946.

Virtual community of practice (VCoP). A group of people who collaborate online, but not in person, regarding similar interests or purposes that affect a specific business unit or group only. VCoPs form unsecured bonds and evolve into groups that promote shared learning and increased understanding among the members[8].

White Paper is an authoritative report giving information or proposals on an issue.

Widget. An application, or a component of an interface, that enables a user to perform a function or access a service.

SOCIAL "COLLABORATIVE" NETWORKING

"On engagement, we're already seeing that mobile users are more likely to be daily active users than desktop users. They're more likely to use Facebook six or seven days of the week."

Mark Zuckerberg, Founder, Facebook

THE ALLURE TO SOCIAL MEDIA

Social media offers many valuable capabilities beyond sharing a great selfie. Individuals worldwide, from nearly every cultural background take time from their busy schedules to participate in social media to keep up-to-date with their friends or family. It is a newly evolved form of socialization, and what once emerged to be a fad, is only gaining momentum. Though platforms like Twitter, Instagram, Pinterest, YouTube, and LinkedIn are rising in popularity, Facebook remains by far the most popular social networking tool, according to findings conducted by the Pew Research Center. The popularity of social media is increasingly multi-generational and multi-cultural. What motivates people to become so captivated by this new form of socialization? Perhaps one reason Facebook is so popular is that it provides a portal into a world without borders. Think about it, before social media, what other avenues offered you the ability to instantly locate and interact with others from around the globe? Social networking uses interactive applications to find, connect, and interact with those who share similar interests. Joining a social media group with similar interests expands that group's knowledge base tremendously.

Corporations are now working to harness the fascination of social media to improve workforce collaboration. Social media has proven to be a great marketing tool for business. The use of corporate social networking—or interpersonal networking online via social media platforms—to promote products and services is steadily increasing. One likely reason is consumers' attraction to social media and the results gained by social media advertising. Corporate use of social networking platforms has expanded the perceptibility of company products and services[17]. Currently, social media users focus primarily on marketing, connecting with family and friends, and communicating with groups of similar interests. Yet the allure of social networking continues to rise, with more robust collaboration tools introduced each year. For instance, corporate recruiters are now using social media as a platform for attracting and retaining new college graduates as employees.

The 7 Fundamentals to Create and Sustain a Successful Knowledge Sharing Organization explores Enterprise SocNet used by Aerospace Inc., to deliver online collaboration capabilities to employees and partners. Enterprise SocNet was designed to provide Aerospace Inc. with a primary communication forum available to employees located internationally. This internally developed tool leverages JavaScript and open frameworks that adhere to World Wide Web Consortium (W3C) standards and other open standards, which allowed it to be customized for workforce needs. For identity management and authentication, Enterprise SocNet is integrated with a commercial product, an enterprise-wide Web single sign-on tool to authenticate user access.

SOCIAL CAPITAL

Social networking is the use of interactive online applications (often social media platforms) to find, connect, and interact with others who share similar interests. Social networking has permeated people's day-to-day lives, becoming an important avenue of computer-mediated communication[18]. The attraction to social networking for personal connection has caught the attention of corporate leaders as a new method of workforce collaboration and knowledge sharing.

The functionality of social networking is similar to a set of actors (the dots) together with the set of connections (the lines) representing a relationship or absence thereof between actors. The actors and the corresponding connections can be depicted in the form of a network diagram, as indicated in Figure 2.

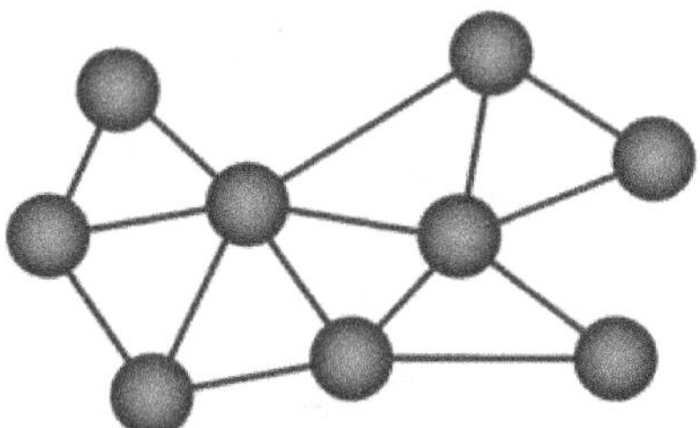

Figure 2. Social networking diagram represents connection.

The theory of social networking unites three types of networks:

1. Egocentric networks, which use one-to-one network-sharing connections.

2. Open-system networks, which are many-to-many, network systems targeting large populations such as corporations or nonprofit organizations that network without identifying structure or boundaries.

3. Socio-centric networks, which are one-to-many network system designed with structure and purpose, such as an organizational network that focuses on workplace issues or concerns and sharing concepts to find a solution.

These various networkings are similar in the sense that they have made a connection to exchange or collect information that is available for their network, commonly known as social capital, as depicted in Figure 3.

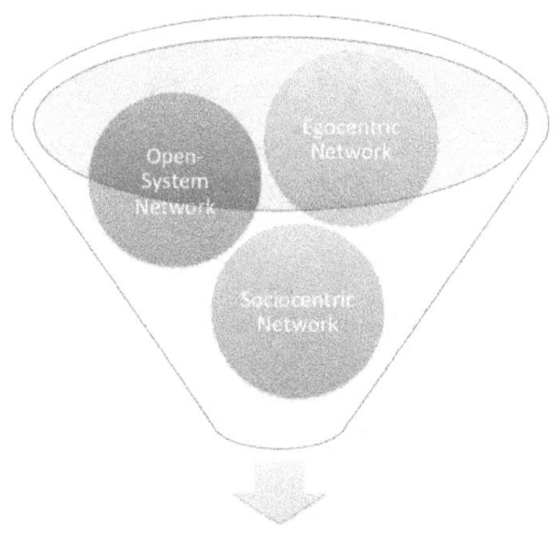

Social Capital

Figure 3. Social capital gained through network interactions.

For virtual groups that use social networking as the primary source of communication, the social capital gained by users is a result of the interactions conducted by the group. According to Maksl and Young, individuals earn social capital as they accrue access to information or emotional support through their relationships with others in the social network[19]. Aligning social network theory with the way in which today's corporate workforce views and utilizes social media may shed light on ways to implement social networking more efficiently within a corporate environment.

The theory of social networking emphasizes the concept of social capital: groups that use social networking as their primary source of communication and collaboration gain social capital through the interactions and knowledge shared within the group[20]. Members of social networking groups also expand their social capital independently as they accumulate access to information through their relationships with other group members. Today, advances in technology and, most notably, social media, have contributed to an ever-changing and competitive world. In this world, it is impossible for an employee or an organization to remain relevant without up-to-date knowledge for resolving continually emerging customer problems and demands for innovative solutions[21]. Some sort of database or library to house knowledge for historical reference and comparisons becomes essential.

THE STIGMA OF SOCIAL MEDIA

Collaborative technology that provides employees with a virtual presence is essential for those who are part of a large workforce; it makes it possible for coworkers to connect with one another. Locating corporate talent is one of the best-known functions of Enterprise SocNet. Enterprise SocNet is structured as a collection of modular widgets that tap into various business systems. These widgets allow users to find people and data throughout the company as well as to broadcast and respond to requests for information. The more details that Enterprise SocNet users add to their profile, the easier it becomes to find coworkers with the skills needed, so employees recognize the value of maintaining a thorough personal profile. Another popular activity is posting questions in the Enterprise SocNet forum. This feature provides an opportunity for employees to crowdsource feedback relative to corporate processes, internal procedures, technical issues, and other topics. Through Enterprise SocNet, employees are also better able to join groups and conduct virtual conversations, whatever their physical location. Employees can also voice opinions and share information by linking to external articles, white papers, videos, or posts from other groups.

At the time that Enterprise SocNet was designed, Facebook was flourishing. According to a Pew Research Study[22] Facebook usage and engagement was on the rise while adoption of other platforms was holding steady. Consequently, modeling Enterprise SocNet capabilities after Facebook seemed logical due to the familiarity of the interface. Still, with the Facebook template comes the stigma associated with Facebook: that it is a platform to connect and socialize. Wagner reviewed a research study on the use of corporate social networking to help professionals share knowledge. In that study, rather than using the term *social networking*, the term *collaborative media* was preferred, to help employees to relate to and understand the tool from a different perspective[23]. This term conveys knowledge sharing through media, which can help an organizational workforce adopt collaborative tools as a knowledge sharing strategy.

Introducing Enterprise SocNet as "social networking" may not have been the best approach. The highest functionality of social media is when it is able to function as an organic environment. Enterprise SocNet was designed to resemble Facebook for ease of use. However, the comparison to Facebook creates the illusion that Enterprise SocNet is primarily a fun social networking tool used for social purposes.

The stigma associated with social media hinders user adoption of Enterprise SocNet, and lack of executive support enforces that stigma. Feedback from VCoP group leaders indicates that the group who created and developed Enterprise SocNet is a small information systems team. The group leaders questioned the reasoning behind retaining such a small team rather than expanding the team to develop the enhancements needed to create a world-class collaborative media tool. For instance, developing a more intuitive user interface, similar to a smartphone interface, would allow employees to choose from among specific icons, each representing a different Enterprise SocNet function or resource. Finally, to help eliminate the stigma associated with Enterprise SocNet, during the planning phase of the next-generation tool, more emphasis should be placed on the collaboration process the tool provides, and less emphasis on the social aspects.

Designing a social networking system similar to out-of-the-box systems may seem like a logical approach, but the similarity may share the stigma associated with the tool. Perhaps using a different title to describe the tool such as "Collaborative Media" would be a better introduction to the workforce.

FINDINGS ON SOCIAL MEDIA USAGE

Responses gathered from VCoP group leaders interviewed to address enhancements to Enterprise SocNet basic functionality are as follows:

- "Integrate Enterprise SocNet with other standard company tools such as Outlook and SharePoint to give users enhanced formatting capabilities and the conveniences other programs provide."

- "After new features are added to Enterprise SocNet, it will be necessary to develop a fresh marketing approach that focuses more on how the tool can be used to benefit employees' careers and organizational successes as well as the long-term benefit to the future of the company."

- "Expand the Enterprise SocNet information systems development team to enhance Enterprise SocNet's capabilities. The current team is relatively small, and investment in a larger team with more social media experience may help bring Enterprise SocNet to the next level."

- "Enterprise SocNet needs real-time data analytics to help provide the critical indicators needed for managers to make quick decisions. The current design offers the ability to communicate and collaborate globally, but no measurement of return-on-investment."

Enterprise SocNet has evolved, but improvements need to be made for users to understand alternative ways to use it. Although many highly populated Enterprise SocNet groups exist within the company, the number of employees who collaborate with a given crowd is relatively small. Another challenge is that some individuals want to create a group under the mistaken notion that the group will organically flourish without any effort by the group leader. A social media platform is a promising tool for improving business outcomes. Yet, the initial phase of identification and control is crucial to instituting a system that works habitually without the need to formally encourage participation[24].

VIRTUAL
COMMUNITIES OF PRACTICE

"For good ideas and true innovation, you need human interaction, conflict, argument, and debate."

Margaret Heffernan, CEO and Entrepreneur

LEARNING THROUGH VIRTUAL COMMUNITIES OF PRACTICE (VCOP)

The theory of organizational learning embodies the processes used to create, retain, and transfer knowledge within an organization and the effectiveness of how those processes help an organization improve over time. Education, training, and work experience combine to foster corporate learning. Knowledge development relies on both individual and team learning[9]. Social media within a workforce environment opens a new avenue for acquiring and sharing knowledge.

A socio-centric—or social-group-centered—network operates as a one-to-many networking system designed with structure and purpose. An organization's commitment to launch such a communication system requires planning, doing, and acting on a process until a measurement of return on investment validates the effort's success[25]. Aerospace Inc. is using VCoPs to enhance corporate knowledge sharing and management. Past research has assessed the value of social networking tools as centralized communication systems for virtual groups such as a VCoP. A VCoP is a group of people who collaborate online, regarding similar interest or purposes with long-term plans for knowledge retention and management. Members of VCoPs form unsecured bonds and evolve into groups that promote shared learning among group members. Aerospace Inc. uses Enterprise SocNet for VCoP communication and collaboration. Enterprise SocNet allows employees in these communities to connect and collaborate for knowledge sharing and problem-solving globally. Survey studies have discovered the more frequently employees shared knowledge via social networking, the more regularly they engaged in learning activities. The experiences and expertise collected through social media or other collaborative technology develop a repository of knowledge that anyone in the workforce can use as a resource or historical library to be used for future study.

The collection of data captured within a VCoP should be maintained and organized in a searchable manner. Filieri and Alguezaui[26] found that failure to establish a process for curating knowledge for long-term use and credibility will hinder participation in the knowledge sharing process. VCoPs that use social networking as their primary collaboration tool can increase organizational learning if the appropriate methodologies are developed and executed[27]. Social media applications such as wikis, blogs, and social networking sites can dramatically change organizational culture through internal social networking communities that foster collaboration and knowledge sharing.

Social networking produces relationship bonding and bridging by introducing individuals to newly formed groups. Egocentric (one-to-one) networks eventually form into socio-centric (one-to-many) networks that broaden the knowledge sharing base. As a VCoP develops, the breadth of knowledge sharing within the group increases, ultimately fostering organizational learning. According to Hotho, scholars who hypothesize about corporate education often rely on literature surrounding organizational learning and knowing[28].

PROCESS VIRTUALIZATION THEORY

In today's corporate world, digital technology used for communication and collaboration is commonplace. Processes once conducted in a brick-and-mortar environment are now undertaken virtually, an activity known as *Process Virtualization.* To provide you with an example of how process virtualization is being used in corporations today, say a corporate IT employee developing a web application experiences difficulties generating the appropriate code to connect a website to a Structured Query Language (SQL) database. Traditionally, the employee would seek assistance from IT co-workers located within their own brick-and-mortar location in what would be considered one-to-one interaction. Alternatively, if the employee became a member of an SQL-focused VCoP, they could then post their question on the SQL VCoP social networking discussion board, which might generate some possible solutions from SQL experts, located globally, in what would be considered a one-to-many interaction. In this case, the user relies on a virtual forum established for the purpose of remote information sharing. Process virtualization plays a crucial role and is an essential process for successfully implementing a social networking forum within a VCoP.

There are four major components of process virtualization theory: (a) sensory requirements, (b) relationship requirements, (c) synchronism requirements, and (d) control and identification requirements. Process virtualization theory postulates that the extent to which a process can be virtual depends on these requirements[29]. In implementing social networking within a VCoP, all four components work together to ensure successful process virtualization.

To enhance collaboration within a discussion forum, sensory requirements are necessary to blur the lines between reality and virtual reality. For instance, internal social networking systems require users to complete personal profiles, including a photo and all professional and personal information, with the aim of creating an increasingly realistic virtual presence. Furthermore, users can conduct regular virtual meetings using Skype or Adobe Connect as a companion tool to stimulate collaboration on the social networking site. At the end of each session, identifying action items or tasks with expected completion dates helps group members maintain a steady collaborative momentum. Implementing this kind of synchronistic process integrates the sensory requirements of virtualization into the process and encourages social networking participants to collaborate and share ideas.

Over time, socio-centric networking patterns develop between individuals with like-minded interests, allowing relationships to organically mature. Although this is the ideal outcome of employing social networking to improve business outcomes, a phase of control and identification is initially vital to establish a foundation that works without the continual need to encourage participation. The first step of implementing a new communication tool such as social networking in a global company requires a steering committee to help develop strategic methods to motivate the workforce to embrace the change in communication. One challenge is that conventional means of communication, such as e-mail, cell phones, and instant messaging, are still thriving within the corporate workforce[24]. These communication methods fragment conversations and do not foster an environment of knowledge sharing and mentorship[30].

As globalization has led to an increase in virtual societies, and many processes once conducted physically are now undertaken virtually, the theory of process virtualization has evolved. Remote communities are of benefit to global corporations, and VCoPs are used to capitalize on the valuable distributed knowledge and to improve workforce collaboration by fully engaging in its innovation potential.

When conducted efficiently, over time, VCoPs form unsecured bonds and evolve into groups that promote shared learning and increased understanding among their membership[8]. Achieving this in a workplace setting is challenging due to the variety of communication styles and practices, fragmented business functions, and geographic dispersal of the VCoP's members. The complexities involved in generating a plan to encourage knowledge sharing via social networking within a corporate VCoP requires long-term commitment and a strategy to keep the momentum going. To achieve appropriate implementation, corporate executives must support creative organizational strategies. Organizations are advised to first recognize the commitment required for a well-developed knowledge-management system before attempting such an effort. In order to effectively establish successful VCoP through process virtualization, executive sponsorship, a steering team committee with a long-term vision, effective virtual collaboration tools, and VCoP group leaders who encourage dialog within group forums are required, as identified in Figure 4.

Figure 4. Virtual Community of Practice using Enterprise SocNet.

Fletcher suggested that the quality relationships nurtured by communities such as VCoPs, in conjunction with productive dialogue, are critical elements to organizations that require constant innovation[31]. Once such a community is launched, the challenge becomes collecting, managing, and sharing information through a knowledge management system to subsequently measure long-term success through documented best practices.

VIRTUAL COMMUNITIES OF PRACTICE AND KNOWLEDGE MANAGEMENT

The ultimate goal of an organization-sponsored VCoP is to establish a knowledge-management resource. Knowledge-management applications are used in organizations that range from small companies to large multinational corporations, and from profit-based to nonprofit organizations[32]. Hundreds of VCoPs currently exist among workers at Aerospace Inc. A large amount of knowledge could be shared if all their communication methods were funneled through Enterprise SocNet, allowing groups of individuals to learn through a stream of conversation. Centralizing discussion is a great way to tap into a flow of knowledge sharing outside of the borders created by traditional methods of communication. By integrating social media within organizational VCoPs, companies can begin to develop a foundation to address the constraints created by traditional methods of communication, with the long-term goal of establishing a progressively interactive social networking interface.

According to Bardon and Borzillo, communities of practice (which include VCoPs) increase organizational learning and innovation because members share and develop knowledge and new practices together on a voluntary basis. These communities, however, cannot be left fully autonomous[33]. Success in a community of practice is attributed to decisive leadership and to group dynamics that enable a supportive environment[34]. For VCoPs, developing a steering committee to help establish and drive the components involved in process virtualization is a necessary element to achieve long-term success. In addition, to acquiring support from corporate executives, a VCoP steering committee must prove success through a measurable return on investment. One method of accomplishing this is for VCoPs to document best practices and lessons learned within a knowledge-management system housing innovations and data that could identify long-term trends to be used for future research.

FINDINGS ON CHALLENGES TO INFLUENCE SOCNET PARTICIPATION

Responses gathered from VCoP group leaders interviewed to address the challenges faced and recommended strategies to influence involvement within Enterprise SocNet, are as follows:

- "If posts made on Enterprise SocNet discussion forums are not entirely correct or in line with either policy or practice, there is always an opportunity for others to comment or rebut. VCoP group leaders can try to be proactive by reviewing posts for data credibility."

- "Managers and executives could be more involved in promoting Enterprise SocNet and the ways it could benefit work-related activities. Managers' interest could change the general mindset about Enterprise SocNet to seeing it as "productive collaboration time" rather than just "social time.""

- "Before someone becomes a VCoP group leader, an orientation session that educates the prospective leader on the long-term commitment involved in administering a social networking group is necessary."

- "When group leaders receive e-mails or phone calls in response to an Enterprise SocNet post, they should direct the person responding to continue the conversation within Enterprise SocNet instead of moving it to other methods of communication, such as responding back to the person via email. The idea is to centralize the discussion to provide all group members with the entire story."

- "VCoPs need to consider varied time zones when conducting meetings. If regular meetings are recorded and posted on Enterprise SocNet, international members can view the knowledge shared during those meetings and follow up with questions later."

- "Social networking is considered the new virtual water cooler used to share dialogue. Group leaders of VCoPs need to formulate a process to identify the pockets of useful information beneficial to the company and archive that info within a knowledge-management system for future reference."

- "It is helpful to develop a small steering team committee for each VCoP group to help establish a knowledge sharing trajectory for the community. Each year, new members should be recruited."

- 'Launching an application process for new groups and group leaders would help avoid the creation of new VCoPs by leaders who are merely seeking recognition or higher visibility from management and do not have the necessary long-term commitment. Manager or executive sponsorship of each new group should be required."

- "VCoPs help bring like-minded employees together to share ideas. Yet, to improve the integrity of the information shared, a data curator role should be established for each community. This can be a different person from the group if the leader does not have the time or inclination to assume that role."

- "VCoP group leaders post questions within their forum regularly to keep the momentum going. Some leaders also send monthly e-mails to those who are not using Enterprise SocNet to share exciting topics discussed in hopes of recruiting more members."

- "No organizational funding charge lines are used for leading a VCoP; this activity is strictly on a volunteer basis. Providing a funding charge line for time spent leading VCoP groups would be a good incentive and a worthy investment for long-term sustainability."

- "Each quarter, the company provides knowledge sharing awards to communities that have enhanced business success through collaborative knowledge sharing and contributions to the long-term continuity of knowledge."

Developing a VCoP is a long-term commitment. Ensuring successful knowledge sharing within a social networking group requires strong leadership involvement to assist in developing and implementing strategic methodologies and long-term sustainable goals[35]. The use of Enterprise SocNet alone is beneficial, by connecting a global workforce in a centralized location. Conversely, organizing how the information benefits the company long-term becomes the role of the VCoP group leaders and steering committees. Organizations have enhanced VCoPs by applying designated steering team committees, which help develop strategies to drive a global workforce toward engagement, collaboration, and knowledge sharing[36].

VCoPs are still considered a relatively new initiative, and determinations on whether a successful VCoP encourages knowledge sharing within a shifting workforce have yet to be made[61]. However, current research indicates that successful knowledge sharing will require high-level social networking strategies, leadership involvement, and alignment of corporate initiatives with VCoP goals. Today, several hundred VCoPs exist in Aerospace Inc. An understanding of the long-term commitment involved is essential for those selected as group leaders. Interviewing a potential leader about his or her long-term vision for the group and how it will benefit the company should be mandatory. Furthermore, management and executive approval and sponsorship of VCoP group leaders should be standard practice, to help bring greater awareness to community interests. Conventional communication methods can be used to help educate executives on the intentions of a VCoP and why collaborative technology benefits the company.

Integrating knowledge-management systems and social networking forums through VCoPs that use social networking can provide a company with valuable insight into its long-range goals and how those goals improve the corporate business value. Ultimately, business outcomes, lessons learned, and documented best practices produce social capital metrics that can be used to measure the success of each community[37].

ORGANIZATIONAL LEARNING

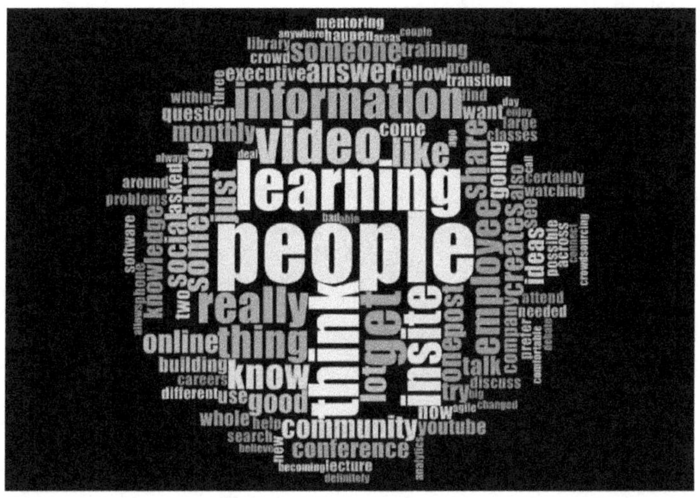

**"Tell me and I'll forget,
teach me and I'll remember,
involve me and I'll learn."**

Benjamin Franklin, The First American

THE FOUR PILLARS OF ORGANIZATIONAL LEARNING

A learning and development formula developed back in the 1980s called the 70-20-10 learning model is commonly used by Corporate America. Morgan McCall and the Centre for Creative Leadership conducted research, which determined 70% of learning comes through job experience (informal learning), 20% through developmental relationships, and 10% through traditional education or training (formal learning). Organizational learning is dependent on both individual and team learning. According to Kroon et al., participation in workforce dialogue and inquiry directly relates to individuals' learning on the job; engagement in social media could stimulate work-related learning[10]. This socially influenced innovation process surfaces during interactions among individuals who are involved in dialogue and the exchange of ideas via social networking[38].

Today, social media and emerging technologies are transforming the traditional 70-20-10 learning model into the four pillars of learning:

1. Experiential learning—Training and learning in the workplace.

2. Referential learning—Organizational coaching or mentoring.

3. Formal learning—Academic and training.

4. Relational learning—Learning through social networking.

See Figure 5 for a comparison of the 70-20-10 learning model and the four pillars of learning:

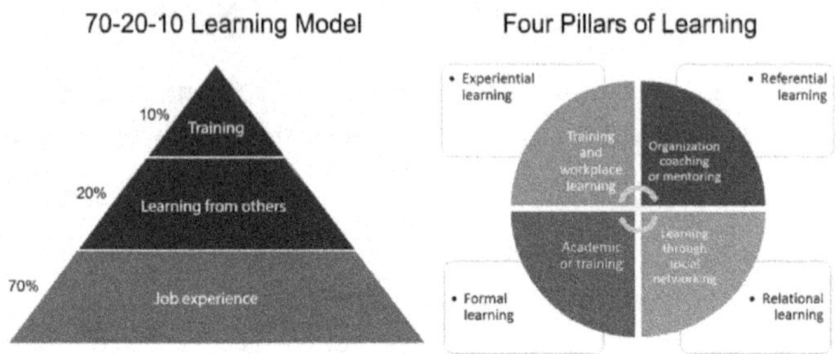

Figure 5. Comparison of the 70-20-10 learning model to the four pillars of learning.

Corporate classroom training has been altered as a result of the attraction to social media. Integrating social media, training videos, lectures, presentations, and online meetings as part of the organization learning process applies various learning styles to extend learning retention. Implementing such a variety of learning methodologies improves workforce learning whether they are auditory – learn through hearing, visual – learn through seeing, or kinesthetic – learn through doing as indicated in Figure 6.

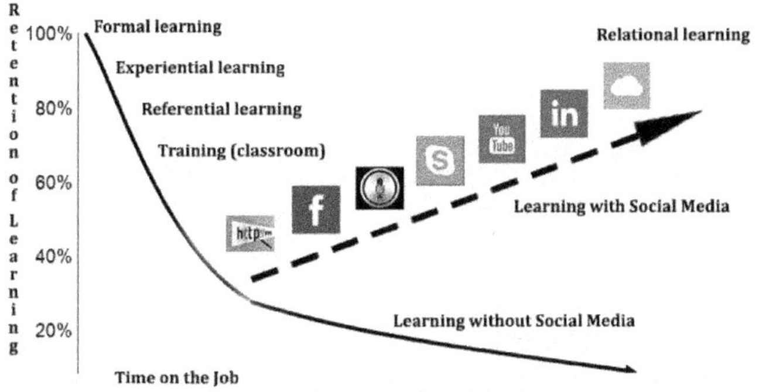

Figure 6. Social media increases learning over time.

Similar to academic learning environments, corporate social networking delivers multiple approaches for sharing information that may be valuable to the workforce. Workforce social networking provides organizations with new opportunities for employee development. Kroon et al.'s study surveyed 590 respondents from three Netherlands-based multinational corporations to investigate the relationship between learning activities accepted by employees and the use of social media. The researchers anticipated that an organization's employees would perceive higher levels of learning when stimulated by dialogue and inquiry via social media. The survey results showed that the more frequently employees shared knowledge via social networking; the more frequently they engaged in learning activities. "The perception of a culture of dialogue and inquiry directly related to learning on the job. The findings suggest that organizations could consider stimulating the use of social media among employees to support work-related learning[10]."

MULTI-GENERATIONAL AND MULTI-CULTURAL LEARNING

Off-the-shelf technological collaboration tools or internally developed tools like Enterprise SocNet can organically alter organizational culture through ongoing virtual discussions. Although such studies are beginning to flourish, researchers have found that these collaborative technologies often do not blend harmoniously with traditional corporate cultures[39]. More scholars are now studying the significance of conducting organizational learning through activities. According to Kroon, Timmerman, Puijenbroek, and Poell, participation in workforce dialogue and inquiry directly relates to increased learning on the job, and social networking could be the answer to stimulating collaborative work-related learning[10]. Additionally, as indicated in Figure 6, Social Media Increases Learning Over Time, further technologies integrated with social media, such as videos, lectures, search capability, presentations, and online meetings, are necessary to produce a more efficient learning environment and increase workforce knowledge retention. The method by which today's workforce learns is shifting, aligning more with the Millennial's adoption of an active and technology-savvy approach to seeking knowledge.

Organizational learning integrates numerous avenues for learning, such as academic learning, corporate training, mentoring, conference attendance, and symposiums. However, these learning options can also be quite costly. Employees are expected to produce trip reports summarizing learning objectives that may be valuable to the company and shared with local colleagues. By using an internal social networking tool, like-minded employees who are globally dispersed can share learning outcomes and relevant white papers, ultimately casting a much broader communication and learning net around the globe.

CROWDSOURCING

A result of social networking, crowdsourcing is a new avenue for acquiring feedback. Employees rely on crowdsourcing and use positive or negative feedback from the crowd as a measurement of their decision-making process. Wikipedia is an excellent example of crowdsourcing. However, assessing the credibility of the data received is a consideration. One leader interviewed provided a great comparison of how the crowdsourcing aspect of social networking works:

> "Suppose you traveled to a new city and you hear about a great restaurant. You look up the restaurant on your smartphone and see it has excellent reviews, so you decide to go there for dinner. When you arrive, you park next to the restaurant but notice there are hardly any cars in the parking lot and the restaurant seems dark and not active at all. Then you look across the street and see another restaurant with many people, and they all seem to be having a good time. You would probably be more likely to go to the busy restaurant to have dinner instead of looking to see if they have an excellent online review because of the crowd. That is how social networking works; people tend to follow the crowd."

WORKFORCE CAREER DEVELOPMENT

As the next generation of employees enters the workforce, they bring knowledge about locating resources and connecting with others online. Aerospace Inc. has created a job-locating website that allows employees to search for positions via job title, location, country, organization, business unit, industry, and skill. The company's social networking tool, Enterprise SocNet, also has a method of locating talent within a group based on the comprehensiveness of an employee's profile; the more detailed the profile, the easier it is to find the talent via keyword search.

Enterprise SocNet permits employees to connect with one another and to discover mentorship opportunities. One section located in the employee profile authorizes employees to advertise themselves as mentors who act as teachers to help less experienced employees. Alternatively, they can promote themselves as mentees or as protégés who would like to break into a different field or advance within their current field. Being mentored also allows an employee to test the waters before committing to an alternative career path. Enterprise SocNet is an excellent resource for identifying specific technical areas for employees who are interested in learning more about those areas.

FINDINGS FOR ORGANIZATIONAL LEARNING

Responses gathered from VCoP group leaders interviewed to address the factors they believed would fuel organizational learning within Enterprise SocNet are as follows:

- "The Enterprise SocNet "Share It" and "Ask It" capabilities are used to market classes, conferences, and symposiums to broaden employee attendance."

- "YouTube videos are a useful resource, and Enterprise SocNet has a related feature, called InVideo, that is similar to YouTube and allows employees and managers to share news, training, how-to, and lessons-learned videos."

- "Social networking creates an exchange, with the building of ideas, debate, contradiction, and innovation. Social networking mixes learning with socialization and offers an alternative learning method for those who may be uncomfortable sharing in other venues."

- "The popularity of crowdsourcing is increasing, and "Ask It" was developed to target the crowd for answers or feedback. Today, the opinion of the crowd counts."

- "The use of social networking increases learning from a local to a national to a global scale. Social networking casts a broader learning net and aligns with how the millennial generation expects to learn."

- "Social networking enhances people's ability to find and establish virtual mentorships, giving employees the option to test the waters of new careers before committing to a change."

- "Enterprise SocNet is the best tool the company has for integrating data from different groups and locations. It is also a career development tool that allows employees to connect with mentors."

- "Although social networking communities allow users to share data, content curators are needed to ensure that the data shared are credible."

- "People trust the crowd, and I think that gets us in trouble because the crowd can be wrong. We just saw an election happen as a result of crowdsourcing. I am not saying that is a good or bad thing; I am telling the predictive analytics that we have always had around knowledge, around social constructs, around all these different things are shifting. The crowd is becoming extremely powerful. If a posting displays on our group site and someone posts an answer, especially if that person has reasonable credibility, their response may be considered the official answer by many people. Unless somebody comes in and challenges a post, you could have some wrong information getting shared."

Enterprise SocNet and VCoP integrate experiential, referential, formal, and relational learning into one common portal[40] as indicated in Figure 5. Technologies often combined with social media include videos, lectures, presentations, and online meetings. These technologies are necessary to produce a more efficient and productive learning environment. Increasingly, scholars are studying the link between organizational learning and improvements in regulatory functions and activities. The shared knowledge at Aerospace Inc. has increased as a result of Enterprise SocNet. Connections made through social networking allow employees to become creatively resourceful. Opportunities to express oneself within a social networking environment also lead to the presence of voices not heard in other venues. The opportunity to learn from others, mentor others, and communicate and collaborate with others bonds a global workforce and ultimately increases organizational learning and retention.

LEADERSHIP PRIORITIES

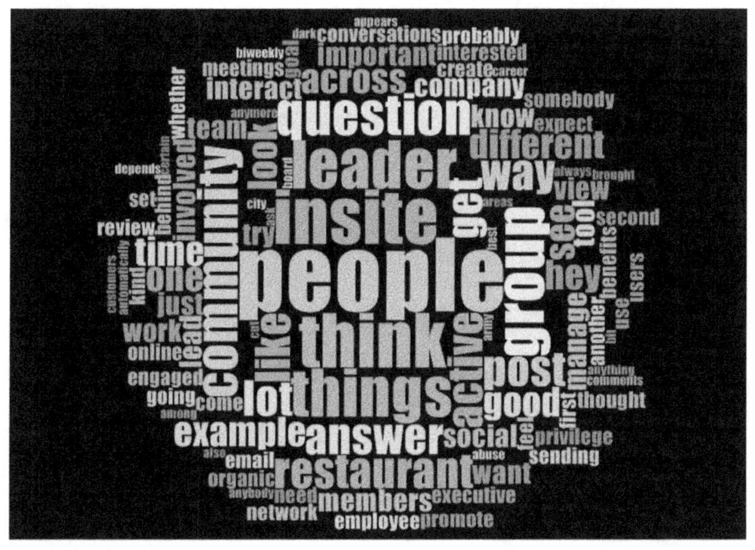

"If your actions inspire others to dream more, learn more, do more, and become more, you are a leader."

John Quincy Adams, U.S. President

LEADERSHIP GOALS

Implementing social media does not, on its own, improve knowledge sharing within a workforce. It is necessary to establish a social networking structure and strategy to encourage knowledge sharing. Progressive knowledge management approaches help create a knowledge sharing culture among staff and generate significant value for the organization by transforming social capital into organized intellectual capital[41].

French explored the communication processes among employees of a consulting organization within a VCoP[42]. The study addressed the advantages and disadvantages of collaboration methodologies, using motivational models of social learning and social capital as the theoretical baseline. The author collected data through in-depth interviews with open-ended questions from 20 participating staff at a small consulting organization in Northern Virginia. This case study's findings indicate that knowledge sharing within the VCoP was successful, but that the collaboration methodologies were not routinely updated. The results were both positive and negative. On the positive side, the organization began to understand how it could use VCoPs to increase efficiency, improve collaboration strategies, and implement positive social change. Other insights involved understanding the various stages of learning within a VCoP:

a) Individuals with similar interests interact using social media.

b) A sense of community begins to evolve, with established goals and norms.

c) Trust between community members begins to form and information sharing increases.

d) Progress and community growth are sustained by developing strategies where necessary.

However, for knowledge to add value to a company, the accuracy of the data is essential. Filieri and Alguezaui, who interviewed 24 research and development employees in the automotive industry sector, found the following:

> "The poor operational quality of a repository hinders knowledge sourcing; thereby, people prefer sourcing knowledge from other colleagues rather than from the repository. Moreover, the inefficiencies in knowledge sourcing from a catalog, the poor quality of the codified knowledge and its complexity affect reusing existing knowledge[26]."

Many social communities exist within organizations, and these communities arguably subsidize organizational knowledge sharing. Within these communities, micro communities of knowledge development and interconnected relationships are formed and maintained, experiences are shared, and ideas are articulated and developed. Fletcher suggested that "the quality of collegial relations fostered by such communities, together with the importance of productive dialogue, have been identified as key components in organizations with the capability for ongoing innovation[33]." Communities of practice evolved into VCoPs as a result of social media. By way of social media, VCoPs create a portal into a community of knowledge sharing and problem-solving. Sustaining the flow of information sharing is key to long-term success of a VCoP, and the strategies used to drive momentum require further research. However, establishing a methodology to house the information that is shared is equally essential, and leadership plays a significant role in creating a knowledge management process that works. According to Cheng and Lee leadership involvement and strategic methodologies are essential to a successful and productive VCoP[43].

LEADERSHIP PERCEPTION OF SOCIAL MEDIA

Group leaders perceive that social media adoption primarily occurs within the younger generation in the workforce. It seems that there is less of a social media learning curve for younger people who have used it for years before entering the workforce. For them, it has become a habit. The older generation still relies on conventional methods of communication to conduct their work and communicate with peers. There seem to be indications that lack of adoption of corporate social media is related to the perception of social media as mainly a tool for socializing. Strategically approaching the use of corporate social media as both serious and beneficial may help remove that stigma.

How do corporate leaders use social media to begin to transition a multigenerational workforce to optimize knowledge sharing and mentorship opportunities, and why is it such a challenge? Many corporations have either failed to anticipate the current generational shift or were unable to establish a plan that works, and they are now struggling to find strategic methodologies to improve communication and collaboration technology, workforce learning, and knowledge sharing.

Meanwhile, as corporations continue to study the value of external, or outward-facing, social media, they are also becoming progressively more concerned with the generational shift in the workforce and the impact it may have on their company. The structure of the workforce is shifting as millennials begin to outnumber baby boomers rapidly. This change presents organizations with a range of challenges and opportunities. According to Jarrahi and Sawyer, research findings on workforce social networking show an increased desire to understand how organizational norms and policies affect the use of social media or collaborative technologies for knowledge sharing[2]. A multigenerational workforce may unintentionally drive use of conventional methods of communicating and sharing knowledge. Although the proportion of tech-savvy millennials in the workforce is steadily increasing, baby boomer and Generation X employees still rely on e-mail, phone, and face-to-face meetings. This forces the millennial workforce to adopt the same tools to obtain feedback or resources from their more-seasoned colleagues.

Ensuring successful knowledge sharing within a social networking group requires leadership involvement. The basic use of Enterprise SocNet within VCoPs has proven compelling enough to draw employee interest in developing professional profiles on the platform. However, to encourage participation and align those discussions with daily workflow requires leadership involvement at all levels.

As the position and attractiveness of social networking surges, across multiple generations, corporate executives should work to encourage their employees to use it as an innovative method of communication for workforce collaboration and knowledge sharing. Leaders need to develop and execute strategic methodologies and long-term sustainable goals to achieve successful knowledge sharing within a social networking group[35]. However, identifying an effective way to do this remains a challenge.

LEADERSHIP INVOLVEMENT

VCoP leaders interviewed for this case study stressed the importance of leading by example. The initial phase of establishing a plan is crucial to instituting a baseline that works habitually without the need to encourage participation[24]. However, in a virtual environment, communication and collaboration rely on a leader to encourage the community's dedication and hard work. Identifying strategic methodologies to drive community members to collaborate in a virtual environment is required for a VCoP to succeed.

Leadership involvement is a crucial indicator of how successful VCoP social networking becomes. Although crowdsourcing is a common practice, leadership involvement and dedication is necessary throughout the initial phase of launching a VCoP social networking environment for the group to grow and prosper organically. Consequently, most VCoPs rely on a long-term commitment from VCoP leaders and steering team members. Leaders must practice methodologies in which employees do not feel pressured but rather persuaded to use social networking regularly.

VCoP leaders use different techniques to foster engagement without appearing to police members. Some methodologies include conducting regular meetings for members to discuss specific issues that may arise, or using those sessions to compare and establish common processes. Additionally, finding ways for new members to better understand how to use the social networking tool seems a common challenge. Changing the current perception of social media may entice the more experienced workforce to realize the benefits it produces.

Many VCoP groups specialize in specific areas, such as software development, career development, or safety. Discussions posted within these groups will have a positive or negative impact on the company, so group leaders need to monitor the feedback on posts and try to encourage others to share their knowledge to improve the credibility of the feedback. Furthermore, if executives are invited to participate within a group, group leaders need to take the initiative to discuss the rules of engagement. For example, group leaders should explain that responding in a commanding manner could hinder dialogue. The ultimate goal is for executives to approach social networking in a manner that levels the playing field between all members of that community, including executives.

FINDINGS FOR LEADERSHIP INVOLVEMENT

Responses gathered from VCoP group leaders interviewed to address how manager or executive involvement in the VCoP group could alter social networking interaction are as follows:

- "Leading by example is crucial to encouraging group participation within a VCoP. The challenging aspect of leading by example is how to drive without members feeling as though they are being policed or forced."

- "When a member joins a social networking group, the system automatically sends an e-mail created by the group leader providing guidance about what the group is for, how to post, and additional resources. This provides the new user with an orientation to Enterprise SocNet."

- "Create visually appealing real-time metrics and data analytics to help group leaders better measure successes and identify areas for improvement."

- "A group leader should set initial requirements for members who ask to join, such as completing a professional profile, and encourage regular use."

- "Managers should practice setting expectations for their team to integrate job-related activities using Enterprise SocNet. Setting expectations helps guide employees to share knowledge and also eliminates the social stigma of Enterprise SocNet being just a fun social forum."

- "When communicating within Enterprise SocNet, executives and managers should practice interacting less authoritatively, to encourage feedback. Levelling the playing field among group members is important: Rather than managers or executives stating, "This is the way it is," state "This is an interesting comment; here are some thoughts." Practice diplomacy."

- "Managers should be proactive about requiring their staff to participate on Enterprise SocNet by using it as a natural resource to complete their daily workflow."

- "Managers should conduct regularly scheduled Enterprise SocNet group meetings and use Enterprise SocNet to address key points highlighted during those sessions."

- "If the use of Enterprise SocNet is related to a job function, there should be a budget to account for the hours spent participating, rather than that work being done on a volunteer basis. Executives should sponsor VCoPs by dedicating a charge line for employees to use."

- "Leaders should avoid posting fortune-cookie or one-size-fits-all comments. Enterprise SocNet members expect real interaction. It is essential to follow through with a post, comment, and reply until the topic is complete. When a manager or group leader disappears during the middle of a discussion thread, it sends the wrong message to group members."

- "VCoP group leaders should be involved in curating content. They should help foster knowledge sharing by harnessing dialogue within the community and verifying the accuracy of data shared."

- "It's useful to ask the community simple questions, such as, "How do you define innovation today?" Asking simple questions allows employees to express their opinions in their context, from their point of view."

- "VCoP group leaders should think of themselves as facilitators who are there to drive as much activity as possible."

- "Educating managers and executives on ways to communicate via Enterprise SocNet and the importance of remaining engaged is vital to the success of this tool. Leaders should remove their managerial hat when participating in Enterprise SocNet, and find a balance between an authoritative and non-authoritative voice. The social media platform should be considered a level playing field for all members to communicate. No bullying or intimidation comments should be allowed."

- "First-level managers need to encourage their workforce to use Enterprise SocNet as a resource and assign employees a goal for their quarterly performance evaluations of demonstrating how they have used Enterprise SocNet for knowledge sharing. Using Enterprise SocNet may not generate success for all employees, but those who do produce an outcome could develop significant ideas toward improved use and usability of the tool. First-line managers should also capture the successes in how Enterprise SocNet has increased knowledge sharing within their groups and, in turn, share those achievements with executives."

- "Midlevel managers could support Enterprise SocNet by providing encouraging, pragmatic responses to posts and making it a habit to visit particular groups on a regular basis to respond or ask questions."

- "Executives should be educated on how the long-term use of Enterprise SocNet benefits the company. Feedback from group leaders indicate that higher-level managers and executives, many of whom belong to older generations, are less likely to use social networking. Providing weekly or monthly success stories may inspire these managers and executives to better understand the benefits of social networking and VCoPs. Successes attributed to Enterprise SocNet may also help convince executives to establish funding a charge line to encourage group leaders to produce more achievements, rather than relying on those leaders to operate on a voluntary basis."

Leadership involvement is one of the keys to influencing participation within a social networking environment[44].

Eliminating the technical intimidation factor is crucial to encouraging user adoption of any tool, and training and repeated use of social networking can help overcome technical intimidation factors. Further, using social networking on a regular basis produces measurable results in the long term. Whether the discussion happening online is positive or negative, managers and executives should execute mindful and optimistic reinforcement when they respond to or engage with a social networking group.

Trust between corporate personnel and leadership is essential and could foster employee mentorship regardless of employee level[45]. Finally, recognition within a social networking group is a great way for group leaders, managers, and executives to encourage member participation and provide affirmation for knowledge shared.

DATA SECURITY

"Security is, I would say, our top priority because for all the exciting things you will be able to do with computers – organizing your lives, staying in touch with people, being creative – if we don't solve these security problems, then people will hold back."

Bill Gates, Microsoft

DATA SECURITY AWARENESS

When a company implements an internal social networking platform, strategic planning is necessary to ensure that employees understand the platform's functionality, any data security concerns, and how sharing knowledge with one another can improve the company's long-term success[46]. Organizational concerns about employees' use of social media—such as concerns related to reputation, privacy, and productivity—are of interest. However, such risks and concerns can be reduced significantly through workforce training, policies, and guidelines[47]. Corporate fears regarding the compromise of data security may remain a major hurdle. Appropriate use of security labeling is vital. For instance, United States employees are not approved to view proprietary data regarding international personnel, and vice versa. Consequently, employees must apply appropriate security labels to social media posts.

Employee concerns regarding sharing proprietary information in the social networking environment may hinder interaction. An employee who unintentionally posts a document labeled "proprietary" or "limited" to a social networking group may create a data security concern for that employee, his or her manager, and the organization itself. Knowledge is a corporation's intellectual capital, essential for gaining a competitive business advantage[48]. Although existing literature supports the need to better understand how corporations benefit from social networking[49], data security awareness in social networking environments remains crucial to protecting company data.

Awareness of the need for data security is prevalent within Aerospace Inc.'s workforce, and employees are required to participate in mandatory information security training. VCoP group leaders indicate that Enterprise SocNet policies and procedures associated with data security are ambiguous, leaving users uncertain how to establish the security needed for specific types of information. Enterprise SocNet notifies users that posts are open to anyone with access to the company's intranet, so users should use appropriate security options relevant to corporate procedures. The following security label buttons are currently available to select when posting on Enterprise SocNet:

1. **U.S. person**—Limits visibility to only U.S. persons.

2. **Employee**—Limits visibility to only those who are considered employees.

3. **Contractor**—Allows visibility to contractors as well as company employees.

4. **Group-limited**—Restricts any content posted within the group to be visible only to members of the group, if the group is set as private.

The following warning notice is available just below the Enterprise SocNet security label buttons:

> "Enterprise SocNet submissions are open to anyone with access to the intranet. Therefore, please use appropriate security options."

THE AMBIQUITY OF DATA SECURITY

Aerospace Inc.'s employees prefer to use Microsoft SharePoint for data sharing, instead of Enterprise SocNet, because of the level and the flexibility of security privileges SharePoint offers. Although the company has existing security policies regarding posting on external social networking sites such as Facebook and LinkedIn, the procedures related to internal workforce social networking are ambiguous. Feedback from group leaders indicate that the security labeling should be less vague, and that it currently adds to the intimidation factor hindering employees from using Enterprise SocNet. Developing a guided user interface and prompting the user to answer specific questions, may help users determine the appropriate security label to use.

Aside from employees and contractors having access to Enterprise SocNet to collaborate and share information, few security features are available to users to help them understand what data should or should not be shared. An employee who is rushing to make a post may not investigate the meaning of each label before posting. The site also references the company policies and procedures resource for further information. Policies regarding data sharing should be reviewed with members of Enterprise SocNet.

SOCIAL MEDIA OPTIMIZES DATA SECURITY AWARENESS

Responses gathered from VCoP group leaders interviewed to address how corporate social media group participation optimize data security awareness and ownership is as follows:

- "Mandatory orientation training on information security should be enforced before a new user begins using Enterprise SocNet."

- "When employees try to "Ask It" or "Share It" within an VCoP community, they should be required to review and choose from a list of data security labels to apply. The current labels are U.S. person, employee, contractor, and group limited."

- "Posts on Enterprise SocNet currently default to being visible to the general population, rather than only to the country in which the author currently resides. A default of posting to local communities would halt the sharing of information with international personnel. Although this practice would enhance data security, it would also segregate knowledge sharing."

- "Leaders should promote company policies related to sharing articles from business magazines such as Forbes, the New York Times, and Entrepreneur to ensure that employees are aware of what violates policy. Company rules and policies should be available on the Enterprise SocNet tool."

- "Enhance clarity regarding different types of

> Enterprise SocNet groups, such as community groups related to hobbies, community groups related to the company's initiatives, and community user groups such as a group focused on programming. The level of security required for a group will be dependent on the topic."

Although data security options are available within the Enterprise SocNet tool, to understand what labels are appropriate and the levels of information security, users must research corporate policies regarding information protection and proprietary information. The company requires employees to participate in mandatory training on information security; still, ambiguity on data labels can leave users uncertain. One method to overcome the intimidation factor related to information security requirements is to create a user interface that guides users through a series of questions concerning the type of data they want to share. Based on the answers given, the system would then direct users to the appropriate level of security needed and the type of security label required.

As an example, an employee would like to seek help from a VCoP programming group on a web application he or she is developing to support the Innovation Organization. The employee will need to provide a detailed description of the web application's purpose for the group to understand how it operates. While posting the inquiry within the VCoP programming discussion forum, the author is prompted with a series of questions before they can proceed with the post:

- **Is the content of this post limited to this group only?**
  Yes or No or Unsure

- **Is the content of this post limited to US persons?** Yes or No or Unsure

- **Does the content of this post restrict Contract Employees?** Yes or No or Unsure

- **Does the content of this post contain EAR/ITAR data?** Yes or No or Unsure

- Etc.

Depending on how the author answers each question, will determine the next inquiry to be prompted. Once the author completes the series of questions, the system will automatically apply the appropriate level of security based on the author's feedback. During this questioning, if the author is unsure how to answer, they will be prompted to discuss the topic with their manager or VCoP Group leader for further clarification.

The need for data security contributes to knowledge hoarding. Employees' unfamiliarity with the level of protection to use may hinder them sharing certain types of data with others, because of security concerns. Ultimately, leaders should encourage knowledge sharing to ensure that the workforce adapts to using Enterprise SocNet without fear of repercussions.

TRAINING THE WORKFORCE

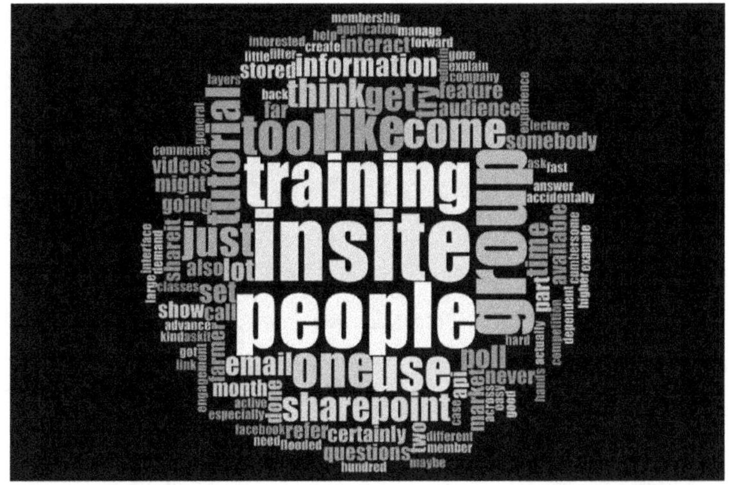

"The only thing worse than training your employees and having them leave, is not training them and having them stay."

Henry Ford, The Ford Motor Company

EDUCATING THE WORKFORCE

Contemporary research has shown that employee values and preferences differ among the generational cohorts in today's changing workforce[50]. Millennials are adapting to a transformation of communication through social media, while seasoned employees prefer more conventional means of communication. The transition from more conventional and one-to-one means of communication such as e-mail, cell phones, and instant messaging to newer and less familiar forums such as social networking groups is not a simple undertaking, particularly for older generational cohorts, such as the baby boomers[14]. The number of millennials in the workplace is growing rapidly, and they will eventually outnumber baby boomers. The types of communication and collaboration tools used in the workplace are thus being re-evaluated to accommodate the needs of a changing workforce.

TRAINING OPPORTUNITIES

Enterprise SocNet has been in existence for over seven years, but many employees misunderstand its actual purpose. Millennials rely heavily on Internet search, social networking, and YouTube videos as resources for learning. Responses received from group leader interviews indicate that although Enterprise SocNet is a valuable tool for global collaboration and knowledge sharing, further improvement and training are necessary for the company to reach maximum learning and collaborating potential. For these developments to occur, executives need to take Enterprise SocNet seriously and should consider additional funding to enhance Enterprise SocNet capabilities. In the interim, VCoP group leaders are forced to find creative ways to train group members and encourage interaction.

When Enterprise SocNet officially launched, there was one introductory video published and available on the Enterprise SocNet welcome page; it provided a brief overview of how to create a professional profile. Since the initial launch of Enterprise SocNet, videos related to establishing a group or poll have developed, and more continue to be developed as requests for training continue. Because the new generation relies heavily on independent research, crowdsourcing, and social collaboration, organizations can benefit by implementing a similar approach into internal social networking tools.

SOCIAL MEDIA ANALYTICS

Group leaders interviewed have been highly successful in implementing methodologies for encouraging social collaboration within their groups, but the interview responses indicate that much improvement could be made to the current Enterprise SocNet tool to reduce the amount of effort involved in leading groups. Further, Enterprise SocNet needs to provide the same capabilities offered by other collaboration tools, such as SharePoint. Today, a method of acquiring a return on investment through analytic reports is a widespread corporate expectation. Developing a robust Enterprise SocNet analytics capability with real-time visual results displayed in a graphical interface would allow groups to see the usability aspects of Enterprise SocNet to forecast future enhancements.

FINDINGS ON SOCIAL MEDIA TRAINING OPPORTUNITIES

Responses gathered from VCoP group leaders interviewed to address if training opportunities on the use of Enterprise SocNet have been offered to VCoP members are as follows:

- "Millennials are familiar with technology. They are resourceful with the Internet, and answers to their questions are just a YouTube search away. The company is also creating a video library to help the workforce learn new things, such as how to use Enterprise SocNet."

- "Adding Application Program Interface (API) capabilities with the Enterprise SocNet environment are recommended. API's are a set of routines, tools, and protocols that specify how software components should interact."

- "Monthly Enterprise SocNet training sessions should be made available to community members."

- "When posting on Enterprise SocNet, tags can be used by the author to identify posts by applying keywords. However, enabling the reader to add a tag at any time enhances search capability. It would be difficult, for the author alone, to anticipate all the search terms employees might use."

- "Enterprise SocNet's functionality should be improved by allowing a share feature for each discussion thread. Also recommended: have all replies stream into one thread to eliminate multiple parallel discussions."

- "Adding more microfeedback mechanisms similar to Facebook's "Like" function is recommended. People enjoy affirmations, which also encourages more dialogue."

- "The ability to integrate and organize files, similar to SharePoint, with editing capabilities, is recommended."

- "An improvement in Enterprise SocNet's metrics is needed. A ready-made graphical interface that provides real-time data analytics to group leaders could deliver return-on-investment to support the tool."

- "The team that developed Enterprise SocNet should be increased in size to help them enhance the tool's collaborative media capabilities."

An organization must first recognize the commitment required for a well-developed knowledge management system before it can achieve an efficient knowledge-management process. Hiring or forming an internal group dedicated to developing Enterprise SocNet social constructs for various group purposes would help encourage both the use of the tool and organization of data.

The use of knowledge management applications is widespread, from small enterprises to large multinational corporations and from profit-based to nonprofit organizations[32]. Enterprise SocNet has proven to be a valuable knowledge-sharing tool for Aerospace Inc.'s social networking groups and VCoPs. However, the initial launch of Enterprise SocNet may have been premature. A research-based orientation on how Enterprise SocNet is used to conduct daily work, the importance of establishing a current Enterprise SocNet profile, and the long-term effects of Enterprise SocNet on knowledge sharing should be required training.

KNOWLEDGE SHARING

"An Investment in Knowledge Pays the Best Interest."

Benjamin Franklin, The First American

KNOWLEDGE HOARDING

Corporate knowledge sharing strategies have become an important issue today. Employees acquire and retain valuable insight over time, and organizations often view the ability of their workforce to share and integrate knowledge efficiently as a competitive advantage. The means by which organizations share knowledge eventually creates core corporate values[51]. Effective knowledge management then conveys knowledge from employees who have it to those who do not, assuming employees are willing to share their knowledge. A survey conducted by corporate employees in China discovered 46% of respondents reported that they had conducted knowledge hoarding at work at least once[52].

According to an article titled "Overcoming Cross-Cultural Barriers to Knowledge Management Using Social Media" smart organizational leaders are increasingly moving toward promoting problem-solving by reducing the barriers between the individual available information[53]. Jain described why this is important:

> "As an organization grows, vested interests assume predominance over organizational interest. This mindset leads to the predominance of hoarding of knowledge over its sharing; conflict over cooperation; group over team; fear over the trust. What was a single entity earlier now takes the shape of a segregated community[54]."

Research on social media systems has indicated that some tools can mitigate cultural barriers to knowledge sharing. Such tools include blogs, social media, and wikis. Thus social networking may be the key to changing an organization's knowledge-hoarding culture. However, shifting the workforce mindset can be challenging. While external knowledge transfer in business communities takes place for the most part among those who implicitly share an interest in a particular practice, a division of work within a company presents strong barriers to internal knowledge transfer[55].

The history of corporate downsizing has a direct effect on employee attitude. Although knowledge hoarding still exists within Aerospace Inc.'s workforce, there appears to be a cultural shift from the old-style mentality of hoarding knowledge to save one's job to a new kind of viewpoint regarding knowledge sharing. When employees share knowledge and experiences, a company becomes more innovative, stronger, and more competitive. When employees are not sharing knowledge, a company is set up for failure. Processes need to be set in place to ensure that knowledge sharing is a priority and an activity through which employees feel rewarded, not punished.

According to a Pew Research Center study, *2018 Social Media Use*, the popularity of social media such as Facebook is growing. However, this interest is primarily increasing within the millennial generation. This same pattern is also trending with the launch of Enterprise SocNet. Yet, the lack of adoption of a new tool by seasoned employees, combined with knowledge hoarding, hinders the use of Enterprise SocNet. Seasoned employees tend to consider the knowledge gained during their extended careers as assets and are wary of sharing their assets with coworkers. The corporate mentality is that one who gives away one's assets is no longer of value to the company. Today, this mentality is shifting due to job-hopping by Millennials, eliminating the desire to hoard information to protect their position.

MULTIGENERATIONAL WORKFORCE

The surge in workplace generational diversity produces varying viewpoints, philosophies, and proficiencies - all of which can stimulate organizational creativity, innovation, and progress. Nevertheless, the differences between Baby Boomers, Gen Xers, and Millennials can also reveal flaws in engagement and productivity. Understanding the differences between generations can undoubtedly improve communication and collaboration.

Traditionalists "The Silent Generation"

- **Born:** Before 1946
- **Influence:** Parents survived the Great Depression
- **Values:** Hard working, respect authority, and follow the rules.
- **Work Ethic**: Works best as individuals doing their part of a bigger cause[63].

Baby Boomers "Me" Generation"

- **Born:** Between 1946 and 1964
- **Influence:** The American Dream, Experienced Layoffs, Work to Live.
- **Value:** Hard working, integrity, beating the competition, questions everything to improve quality and desire to win.

- **Work Ethic:** Driven, workaholics, created the culture of meetings[63].

Generation X "Post Boomers"

- **Born:** Between 1965 and 1981
- **Influence:** Dual Income Families – Downsizing.
- **Value:** Education, work-life balance, diversity, fun, and think globally.
- **Work Ethic:** Self-reliant, work smarter, less hours, need to be in charge of their own destiny[63].

Generation Y "Millennials"

- **Born:** between 1982 and 2000
- **Influence:** Digital media, raised by single parents, kept busy as kids, terrorism, school shootings, and mass murders.
- **Value:** Mobility, motivated, goal oriented, change for the greater good.
- **Work Ethic:** Multi-taskers, motivated to get tasks done because their goal is to enjoy life as soon as the job is complete[63].

There is a direct correlation between adoption of social media and generational cohort. There was a wide age range among the VCoP group leaders who participated in the interview process for this case study. Although as leaders, they are committed to promoting social networking, their view of the purpose of the social networking tool and their comfort level with using it was varied. There appears to be a consensus that the adoption of social media lies more with the younger generation. Lack of social media use, among those who choose not to engage in social networking, may also have a direct correlation with attitudes towards knowledge hoarding.

CHANGING THE GENERATIONAL MINDSET

Today, a generational shift in the corporate workforce is the dominant driving force for management initiatives that encourage knowledge sharing[56]. Corporations have significant concerns about Baby Boomers and Generation-Xers leaving the workforce and about the consequences of losing the valuable knowledge these employees acquired throughout their careers. Organizations are cognizant of the need to harvest and transfer this knowledge within a knowledge-management system or through an established mentorship program. Existing research, however, provides evidence that employee values and preferences differ among the generational cohorts represented in the current workforce, creating the challenge of bridging the generation gap[50].

Twenty-first-century technological shifts continue to introduce changes in how workers collaborate with one another[57]. Today's workforce is composed of multiple generations whose differences in values, ideas, ways of getting things done, and methods of workplace communication add to the complexity. Within a workforce, generational differences can affect everything including recruiting, retention, building teams, dealing with change, motivating, and managing and maintaining increases in productivity. Aerospace Inc. is striving to establish a process to shift the cultural mindset toward knowledge sharing. Social networking via Enterprise SocNet, together with the implementation of accompanying knowledge sharing initiatives, may be the tool that will help the company accomplish this goal.

The long-term effect of multigenerational knowledge sharing and knowledge transfer is to ensure the sustainability of an effective knowledge-management curriculum[58]. Combining internal corporate social networking with VCoPs can create a process designed to increase collaboration within a global workforce and to help house knowledge gained within a VCoP system[59]. The traditional values of face-to-face communication are changing, and this change is not widely accepted; it is a process of adaptation that requires a long-term commitment to establishing a cultivated knowledge sharing environment.

FINDINGS ON CORPORATE KNOWLEDGE HOARDING

Responses gathered from VCoP group leaders interviewed to address motivational factors that could help reduce workforce knowledge hoarding are as follows:

- "Historically, knowledge hoarding is a behaviour associated with job security; but company attitudes are shifting, and group leaders are motivated to help employees understand how their knowledge can help others."

- "There is a consensus among VCoP group leaders that knowledge hoarding is most common among older generations."

- "Knowledge hoarding is also a result of the intimidation factor associated with actions that have the potential to compromise data security. Creating less ambiguous security labels in Enterprise SocNet, together with prompts to apply security settings before posting could reduce knowledge hoarding."

- 'Knowledge sharing is not always considered positive. Honest feedback is necessary to ensure that the data shared are credible. It is essential for all group members, regardless of the level of their positions, to practice proper etiquette and diplomatic dialogue when challenging a post or responding to a challenge."

- "The company's leaders tend to be older, and older generations are more associated with knowledge hoarding. Lack of interest in Enterprise SocNet among managers and executives may be a result of lack of understanding of collaborative technology, and this environment will ultimately contribute to knowledge hoarding."

- "Employee attitudes, energy level, and level of desire to adopt new tools or interact with others all affect knowledge hoarding."

- "Questions posted on Enterprise SocNet are not always followed up with an answer on Enterprise SocNet. Those who are intimidated by the idea of documenting their opinion on social media for everyone to see may follow up with an e-mail message or phone call instead of a post to the group."

This study found a consensus among social networking group leaders that knowledge hoarding behavior is seen predominantly among older workers due to fear of losing their jobs. These group leaders are trying to encourage employees to share knowledge by focusing on helping others. This is a change in cultural mindset that will take time. Workforce training on the benefits as well as the technical aspects of using social media is seen as vital to the success of Enterprise SocNet. Such training could bring awareness to the long-term value that social networking and sharing knowledge provides to an organization.

The notion that the knowledge hoarding behaviour changes merely because a social networking tool is available is false. The tool may inspire millennials, but not all employees. If the factors that initially fuelled the knowledge-hoarding behaviour still exist—such as downsizing, outsourcing, and reorganizations—it will be difficult to change routines that employee's feel has helped them to retain long-term employment.

SUMMARY

In summary, the challenges faced by Aerospace Inc.'s leaders were discernable and the strategies they use to administer social networking environments while leading VCoPs are pending. Data analytic reports identified the most interactive VCoP groups on the internal Enterprise SocNet platform. Group leaders of those VCoPs, who were also experts in the field of knowledge management, participated in interviews surrounding the use of social networking within their VCoPs. The leaders interviewed provided insights into the effectiveness of corporate knowledge transfer relative to (1) social media usage, (2) challenges to influence SocNet Net participation, (3) organizational learning, (4) leadership involvement, (5) how social media optimizes data security awareness, (6) social media training opportunities, and (7) corporate knowledge hoarding.

Strategies for social networking that company's use today are in their infancy. Adding to the body of knowledge surrounding corporate social networking strategies can contribute tremendous value to social networking theory and to corporations worldwide who implement VCoPs. According to Joyner, "as the importance of creating high engagement workplaces becomes increasingly well quantified, a growing number of organizations strive to implement engagement strategies and initiatives[6]."

Decisions regarding the best corporate collaboration systems often do not take into consideration individuals' (socially derived) perceptions of social technology features. Iglesias-Pradas, Hernández-García, and Fernández-

Cardador revealed through an exploratory study the usefulness of social presence, group support, and perceived compatibility[60]." This study of the implementation of corporate blogs used data from 73 employees to corroborate a grounded theory model. Findings demonstrate that social networking and user values influence a blog's apparent usefulness and play an essential role in its adoption. The study also revealed the importance of executing corporate strategies that encourage participation in social networking.

CONCLUSIONS

Research on corporate social networking has shown there is an increased desire to understand how organizational norms and policies affect the use of social media for knowledge sharing[2]. According to one leader who managed a social networking group, social networking creates an exchange, the building of ideas, debate, contradiction, and innovation. The use of corporate social networking mixes learning with socialization and offers the opportunity to hear voices not heard in other venues. Social networking integrates experiential, referential, formal, and relational learning into one common portal[40]. According to van Puijenbroek, Poell, Kroon, and Timmerman participation in workforce dialogue and inquiry directly relates to learning on the job, and social networking could be the answer to stimulating work-related learning[62]. Technologies integrated with social media, such as videos, lectures, browser searching, virtual presentations, and online meetings, are necessary to produce a more efficient learning environment.

Corporations face the challenge of developing creative strategies to transfer workforce knowledge from seasoned employees to new hires. They are motivated by shifts in the workforce due to layoffs, resignations, retirements, restructuring, and outsourcing[6]. Factors such as these also contribute to employees hoarding knowledge to retain job security[7]. There is a corporate mentality that if one gives away one's assets, one is no longer of value to the company[63]. Corporate leaders are thus struggling to encourage workforce knowledge sharing and are strategically working to develop methodologies to change today's corporate cultural mindset from knowledge hoarding to knowledge sharing[2]. Today's corporations encourage employees to share knowledge by focusing on helping others. This is a mindset change that will take time, and leaders' involvement can help. Leadership involvement is also necessary to successfully transition the workforce from using conventional methods of communicating such as face-to-face, e-mail, or phone conversations to communicating through social networking[35].

Eliminating the intimidation factor is key to encouraging user adoption of any tool. Combining training and regular use of the Enterprise SocNet in work-related activities will help eliminate the technical hurdle, as will an understanding of the long-term benefits social networking can produce. Whether an employee's post is positive or negative, managers and executives should execute mindful and optimistic reinforcement when responding or engaging within a social networking group. Affirmations are a great way for group leaders, managers, and executives to encourage participation.

Finally, if the use of Enterprise SocNet within a VCoP aligns with corporate initiatives, creating a specific funding charge line should be considered. An interview process should be established to hire community leaders to help formulate group steering committees, and the approval process should include managers and executives. Applying these methods could remove the stigma currently associated with the Enterprise SocNet tool and redirect employee perceptions to associate Enterprise SocNet with corporate knowledge sharing initiatives.

When implementing an internal social networking platform, strategic planning is necessary to ensure that employees understand the platform's functionality, the data security concerns, and how sharing knowledge with one another can improve the corporation's long-term success[46]. Although various forms of training are currently available for Enterprise SocNet, the following improvements are recommended: (a) expanding the video library, (b) adding application program interface (API) capability, (c) improving data security labeling process, (d) holding regularly scheduled training sessions, (e) consolidating discussion threads, (f) adding more micro feedback mechanisms similar to emojis to encourage affirmations, and (g) improving the metrics capability to generate real-time data. Meanwhile, the use of Enterprise SocNet continues to rise and enhancements continue to be made. It appears to be a tool that employees are curious about, and that interest may help generate future group leaders to support VCoP best practices in knowledge sharing.

The purpose of this case study was to identify the challenges social networking group leaders face and the strategies they use to promote Enterprise SocNet for collaboration and knowledge sharing within VCoPs. The study showed the complexity involved in changing the process trajectory and the need for executive involvement to help remove the obstacles that hinder workforce involvement in social networking. As corporate digital business strategies continue to evolve, organizations need to understand how innovation, productivity, and collaboration among a multigenerational workforce depend on reliable systems designed to assist in sharing and retaining information, whether developed internally or off-the-shelf. Executives must anticipate how trends in business, society, technology, and information converge to change where, when, why, and with whom we work[1].

Data from this study revealed that group leaders have been successful in using strategies to increase organizational learning and knowledge sharing through VCoPs, and Enterprise SocNet has been instrumental in achieving those successes. Yet, support from executives is needed to address Enterprise SocNet's limitations and transition its VCoP groups from operating on a volunteer basis to becoming fully funded initiatives. Findings indicate that these changes will help increase internal engagement in social media to help drive organizational knowledge sharing. The use of Enterprise SocNet does appear to be growing, and as the social media generation continues to enter the workforce, usability will continue to increase. The goal of VCoP leaders is to harness that knowledge shared within the VCoPs and turn it into a useful resource that benefits Aerospace Inc. long-term.

ADDITIONAL FINDINGS

Additional documents used for this study include artifacts on Enterprise SocNet's purpose and capabilities, a comparative analysis of Enterprise SocNet to off-the-shelf tools, and Aerospace Inc.'s business assessment on the functionality and usability of Enterprise SocNet. Discoveries discussed in this book, and findings from additional artifacts are published in *Workforce Knowledge Sharing Strategies Using Social Media: An Aerospace Industry Case Study* and can be located in the Dissertations and Theses section of ProQuest.com.

REFERENCES

1. Treharne, T. (2017). Inside the digital workplace. *Computer Reseller News*. Retrieved from https://muckrack.com/media-outlet/channelweb

2. Jarrahi, M. H., & Sawyer, S. (2015). Theorizing on the take-up of social technologies, organizational policies and norms, and consultants' knowledge-sharing practices. *Journal of the Association for Information Science & Technology*, *66*(1), 162–179. doi:10.1002/asi.23161

3. Thomas, J., & Akdere, M. (2013). Social media as collaborative media in workplace learning. *Human Resource Development Review*, *12*(3), 329–344. doi:10.1177/1534484312472331

4. Moqbel, M., Nevo, S., & Kock, N. (2013). Organizational members' use of social networking sites and job performance. Information Technology & People, 26(3), 240-264. doi:http://dx.doi.org.library.capella.edu/10.1108/ITP-10-2012-0110

5. Cawsey, T., & Rowley, J. (2016). Social media brand building strategies in B2B companies. *Marketing Intelligence & Planning*, *34*(6), 754-776. doi:10.1108/mip-04-2015-0079

6. Joyner, F. F. (2015). Bridging the knowing/doing gap to create high engagement work cultures. *Journal of Applied Business Research*, *31*(3), 1131–1148. doi:10.19030/jabr.v31i3.9237

7. Mitchell, A. (2012). From data hoarding to data sharing. *Journal of Direct, Data and Digital Marketing Practice, 13*(4), 325–334. doi:10.1057/dddmp.2012.3

8. Dolan, J. J. (2013). *An exploratory examination of social media, informal learning, and communities of practice in the workplace* (Doctoral dissertation). Available from ProQuest Dissertations and Theses database. (UMI No. 1467526102)

9. Açıkgöz, A., Günsel, A., Bayyurt, N., & Kuzey, C. (2014). Team climate, team cognition, team intuition, and software quality: The moderating role of project complexity. *Group Decision and Negotiation, 23*(5), 1145–1176. doi:10.1007/s10726-013-9367-1

10. Kroon, B., Timmerman, V., Puijenbroek, T., & Poell, R. F. (2014). The effect of social media use on work-related learning. *Journal of Computer Assisted Learning, 30*(2), 159–172. doi:10.1111/jcal.12037

11. Nevo, S., Nevo, D., & Kim, H. (2012). From recreational applications to workplace technologies: An empirical study of cross-context IS continuance in the case of virtual worlds. *Journal of Information Technology, 27*(1), 74–86. doi:10.1057/jit.2011.18

12. Lease, M., & Yilmaz, E. (2013). Crowdsourcing for information retrieval: introduction to the special issue. *Information Retrieval, 16*(2), 91-100. doi:10.1007/s10791-013-9222-7

13. Lyons, S., Urick, M., Kuron, L., & Schweitzer, L. (2015). Generational Differences in the Workplace: There Is Complexity Beyond the Stereotypes. *Industrial*

and Organizational Psychology, *8*(03), 346-356. doi:10.1017/iop.2015.48

14. Sinclaire, J. K., & Vogus, C. E. (2011). Adoption of social networking sites: An exploratory adaptive structuration perspective for global organizations. *Information Technology and Management*, *12*(4), 293–314. doi:10.1007/s10799-011-0086-5

15. Muqadas, F., Rehman, M., Aslam, U., & Ur-Rahman, U. (2017). Exploring the challenges, trends and issues for knowledge sharing. *VINE Journal of Information and Knowledge Management Systems*, *47*(1), 2-15. doi:10.1108/vjikms-06-2016-0036

16. Russell, L. R., Parker, J., Bolden, N., & Sherman, H. (2011). Free, cheap, easy and effective: Knowledge management strategies for building a global community of practice. *International Journal of Education and Development using Information and Communication Technology*, *7*(2), 68–77. Retrieved from http://ijedict.dec.uwi.edu/include/getdoc.php?id=4776&article=924&mode=pdf

17. Chow, W. S., & Shi, S. (2015). Investigating customers satisfaction with brand pages in social networking sites. *Journal of Computer Information Systems*, *55*(2), 48–58. doi:10.1080/08874417.2015.11645756

18. Lin, K., & Lu, H. (2011). Why people use social networking sites: An empirical study integrating network externalities and motivation theory. *Computers in Human Behavior*, *27*(3), 1152–1161. doi:10.1016/j.chb.2010.12.009

19. Maksl, A., & Young, R. (2013). Affording to exchange: Social capital and online information sharing. *Cyberpsychology, Behavior and Social Networking, 16*(8), 588–592. doi:10.1089/cyber.2012.0430

20. Razzaque, A., Eldabi, T., & Jalal-Karim, A. (2013). Physician virtual community and medical decision making. *Journal of Enterprise Information Management, 26*(5), 500–515. doi:10.1108/JEIM-07-2013-0047

21. Ghaznavi, M., Toulson, P., Perry, M., & Logan, K. (2013). Organisational learning and problem solving through cross-firm networking of professionals. In A. Green (Ed.), *The Proceedings of the 10th International Conference on Intellectual Capital, Knowledge Management and Organisational Learning* (pp. 177–185). Reading, England: Academic Conferences and Publishing International.

22. Greenwood, S., Perrin, A., & Duggan, M. (2016). *Social media update 2016*. Retrieved from http://assets.pewresearch.org/wp-content/uploads/sites/14/2016/11/10132827/PI_2016.
11.11_Social-Media-Update_FINAL.pdf

23. Wagner, D., Vollmar, G., & Wagner, H. (2014). The impact of information technology on knowledge creation. *Journal of Enterprise Information Management, 27*(1), 31–44. doi:10.1108/JEIM-09-2012-0063

24. Pan, Y., Xu, Y., Wang, X., Zhang, C., Ling, H., & Lin, J. (2015). Integrating social networking support for dyadic knowledge exchange: A study in a virtual community of practice. *Information & Management,*

52(1), 61–70. doi:10.1016/j.im.2014.10.001

25. Juneau, H. L., Thomas, G. R., Nystrom, M., & Muras, A. (2014). Implementing communities of practice in a matrix organization. In S. Long, E.-H. Ng, & C. Downing (Eds.), *Proceedings of the American Society for Engineering Management 2014 International Annual Conference* (pp. 1–10). Retrieved from https://www.slideshare.net/andrewmuras/implementing-communities-of-practice-in-a-matrix-organization-40685579

26. Filieri, R., & Alguezaui, S. (2015). Knowledge sourcing and knowledge reuse in the virtual product prototyping: An exploratory study in a large automotive supplier of R&D. *Expert Systems, 32*(6), 637–651. doi:10.1111/exsy.12101

27. Neufeld, D., Fang, Y., & Wan, Z. (2013). Community of practice behaviors and individual learning outcomes. *Group Decision and Negotiation, 22*(4), 617-639. doi:http://dx.doi.org.library.capella.edu/10.1007/s10726-012-9284-8

28. Hotho, J. J., Lyles, M. A., & Easterby-Smith, M. (2015). The mutual impact of global strategy and organizational learning: Current themes and future directions. *Global Strategy Journal, 5*(2), 85–112. doi:10.1002/gsj.1097

29. Connolly, A. J. (2014). *The use and effectiveness of online social media in volunteer organizations* (Doctoral dissertation). Available from ProQuest Dissertations and Theses database. (UMI No. 1561559474)

30. Hastings, S. O., & Payne, H. J. (2013). Expressions of dissent in email: Qualitative insights into uses and meanings of organizational dissent. *International Journal of Business Communication*, *50*(3), 309–331. doi:10.1177/0021943613487071

31. Fletcher, J. (2014). Social communities in a knowledge enabling organizational context: Interaction and relational engagement in a community of practice and a micro-community of knowledge. *Discourse & Communication*, *8*(4), 351–369. doi:10.1177/1750481314537577

32. Wong, K. Y., Tan, L. P., Lee, C. S., & Wong, W. P. (2015). Knowledge management performance measurement: Measures, approaches, trends and future directions. *Information Development*, *31*(3), 239–257. doi:10.1177/0266666913513278

33. Bardon, T., & Borzillo, S. (2016). Communities of practice: Control or autonomy? *The Journal of Business Strategy*, *37*(1), 11–18. doi:10.1108/JBS-02-2015-0018

34. Edgar, D., Watson, R., Towle, S., McLoughlin, J., & Paloff, A. (2016). Learning to walk the community of practice tightrope. *International Practice Development Journal,* *6*(2), 1–8. doi:10.19043/ipdj.62.009

35. Battistella, C., Annarelli, A., & Nonino, F. (2015). Exploring the impact of organizational and working models, incentives and collaboration strategies on innovation development in online communities of practices. *Proceedings of the European Conference on Knowledge Management* (pp. 112–121). Reading, England: Academic Conferences International Limited.

36. Yan, Y., Zha, X., & Yan, M. (2014). Exploring employee perceptions of Web 2.0 virtual communities from the perspective of knowledge sharing. *Aslib Journal of Information Management, 66*(4), 381–400. doi:10.1108/ajim-08-2013-0070

37. Frick, B. L., & Hoffman, L. C. (2012). It takes two to tango: The use of social network theory in explaining knowledge production through research networks. *South African Journal of Higher Education, 26*(6), 1152–1158. doi:10.20853/26-6-218

38. Pesämaa, O., Shoham, A., Khan, M. L., & Muhammad, I. J. (2015). The impact of social networking and learning orientation on performance. *Journal of Global Marketing, 28*(2), 113–131. doi:10.1080/08911762.2014.991016

39. Koch, H., Leidner, D. E., & Gonzalez, E. S. (2013). Digitally enabling social networks: Resolving IT–culture conflict. *Information Systems Journal, 23*(6), 501–523. doi:10.1111/isj.12020

40. Gaul, P. (2016, March). Training ain't training without the learner. *[Talent Development] TD Magazine*. Retrieved from https://www.td.org/Publications/Magazines/TD/TD-Archive/2016/03/Intelligence-Training-Aint-Training-Without-the-Learner

41. Mojibi, T., Hosseinzadeh, S., & Khojasteh, Y. (2015). Organizational culture and its relationship with knowledge management strategy: A case study. *Knowledge Management Research & Practice, 13*(3), 281–288. doi:10.1057/kmrp.2013.49

42. French, R. C. (2013). *Effects of a virtual community of practice in a management consulting organization* (Doctoral dissertation). Available from ProQuest Dissertations and Theses database. (UMI No. 1353769293)

43. Cheng, C. K. E., & Lee, C. K. J. (2014). Developing strategies for communities of practice. *The International Journal of Educational Management, 28*(6), 751–764. doi:10.1108/IJEM-07-2013-0105

44. Baker-Eveleth, L. J., Chung, Y., Eveleth, D. M., & O'Neill, M. (2011). Developing a community of practice through learning climate, leader support, and leader interaction. *American Journal of Business Education, 4*(2), 33–40. doi:10.19030/ajbe.v4i2.3560

45. Russell, L. R., Parker, J., Bolden, N., & Sherman, H. (2011). Free, cheap, easy and effective: Knowledge management strategies for building a global community of practice. *International Journal of Education and Development using Information and Communication Technology*, *7*(2), 68–77. Retrieved from http://ijedict.dec.uwi.edu/include/getdoc.php?id=4776&article=924&mode=pdf

46. Pawlowski, J. M., Bick, M., Peinl, R., Thalmann, S., Maier, R., Hetmank, L., . . . Pirkkalainen, H. (2014). Social knowledge environments. *Business & Information Systems Engineering, 6*(2), 81–88. doi:10.1007/s12599-014-0318-4

47. Cleary, M., Ferguson, C., Jackson, D., & Watson, R. (2013). Editorial: Social media and the new e-professionalism. *Contemporary Nurse: A Journal for the Australian Nursing Profession, 45*(2), 152–154. Retrieved

from PubMed database. (PMID No. 24422224)

48. Hong, D., Suh, E., & Koo, C. (2011). Developing strategies for overcoming barriers to knowledge sharing based on conversational knowledge management: A case study of a financial company. *Expert Systems With Applications*, *38*(12), 14417–14427. doi:10.1016/j.eswa.2011.04.072

49. Eckenhofer, E. M. (2011). Outlining the benefits of Strategic Networking. *Journal of Systems Integration, 2,* 70–86. doi:10.20470/jsi.v2i4.104

50. Lyons, S., Urick, M., Kuron, L., & Schweitzer, L. (2015). Generational Differences in the Workplace: There Is Complexity Beyond the Stereotypes. *Industrial and Organizational Psychology*, *8*(03), 346-356. doi:10.1017/iop.2015.48

51. Yen, Y., Tseng, J., & Wang, H. (2013). The effect of internal social capital on knowledge sharing. *Knowledge Management Research & Practice*, *13*(2), 214–224. doi:10.1057/ kmrp.2013.43

52. Huo, W., Cai, Z., Luo, J., Men, C., & Jia, R. (2016). Antecedents and intervention mechanisms: a multi-level study of R&D team's knowledge hiding behavior. *Journal Of Knowledge Management*, *20*(5), 880-897. doi: 10.1108/jkm-11-2015-0451

53. Ray, D. (2014). Overcoming cross-cultural barriers to knowledge management using social media. *Journal of Enterprise Information Management*, *27*(1), 45–55. doi:10.1108/JEIM-09-2012-0053

54. Jain, N. (2012). Knowledge hoarding: A bottleneck to organizational success. *Indian Journal of Industrial Relations, 47*(4), 750–752. Retrieved from Business Source Complete database. (Accession No. 82030196)

55. Online corporate social networking. (2012). *Development and Learning in Organizations, 27*(1), 19–21. doi:10.1108/14777281311291240

56. Ragab, M. A. F., & Arisha, A. (2013). Knowledge management and measurement: A critical review. *Journal of Knowledge Management, 17*(6), 873–901. doi:10.1108/jkm-12-2012-0381

57. Wesolowski, P. (2014). Melding a multi-generational workforce. *Human Resource Management International Digest, 22*(2), 33–35. doi:10.1108/hrmid-04-2014-0041

58. Rivers, M. (2015). *Bridging the knowledge gap between the Baby Boomers and the multi-generations* (Doctoral dissertation). Available from ProQuest Dissertations and Theses database. (UMI No. 3547159)

59. Novakovich, J., Miah, S., & Shaw, S. (2017). Designing curriculum to shape professional social media skills and identity in virtual communities of practice. *Computers & Education, 104*, 65–90. doi:10.1016/j.compedu.2016.11.002

60. Iglesias-Pradas, S., Hernández-García, Á., & Fernández-Cardador, P. (2014). How socially derived characteristics of technology shape the adoption of corporate Web 2.0 tools for collaboration. *Service Business, 8*(3), 465–478. doi:10.1007/s11628-014-0250-1

61. Bandow, D., & Gerweck, J. T. (2015). Support your local communities of practice. *Development and Learning in Organizations: An International Journal, 29*(5), 7–9. doi:10.1108/dlo-11-2014-008

62. Van Puijenbroek, T., Poell, R., Kroon, B., & Timmerman, V. (2013). The effect of social media use on work-related learning. *Journal of Computer Assisted Learning, 30*(2), 159–172. doi:10.1111/jcal.12037

63. Ford, D., Myrden, S. E., & Jones, T. D. (2015). Understanding "disengagement from knowledge sharing": Engagement theory versus adaptive cost theory. *Journal of Knowledge Management, 19*(3), 476–496. doi:10.1108/jkm-11-2014-0469

64. Waschek, M. (2017, November 3). *Understanding Generational Differences in the Workplace.* Retrieved from https://www.croplife.com/management/understanding-generational-differences-workplace/

65. Schlagwein, D., & Bjørn-Andersen, N. (2014). Organizational learning with crowdsourcing: The revelatory case of LEGO. *Journal of the Association for Information Systems, 15*(11), 754–778. Retrieved from http://aisel.aisnet.org/cgi/viewcontent.cgi?article=1693&context=jais

66. Percy, W. H., Kostere, K., & Kostere, S. (2015). Generic qualitative research in psychology. *The Qualitative Report, 20*(2), 76–85. Retrieved from http://nsuworks.nova.edu/tqr/vol20/iss2/7/

LIST OF FIGURES

ABOUT THE AUTHOR

Dr. Patricia Pedraza-Nafziger is a self-proclaimed "geek girl" with a passion for technology, learning, and teaching. As an information systems team leader with a demonstrated history in the aerospace industry, Patricia has gained a wealth of experience. Her goal as a College Professor is to share her knowledge to simulate a positive influence on the academic development of the next generation. To learn more visit: http://www.PatriciaPedrazaNafziger.com

www.ingramcontent.com/pod-product-compliance
Lightning Source LLC
LaVergne TN
LVHW010922110826
845149LV00013B/2453

* 9 7 8 0 9 8 9 9 0 4 2 2 3 *